WHITE ROSE
CHALLENGE WALK

by Darryl Dawson

The White Rose Challenge Walk links two well-known land marks - *'The White Horse of Kilburn'* and *'Roseberry Topping'*. Much of the walk is along the Cleveland Way through the western escarpment of the Hambleton and Cleveland Hills.

"without challenge there is no achievement"

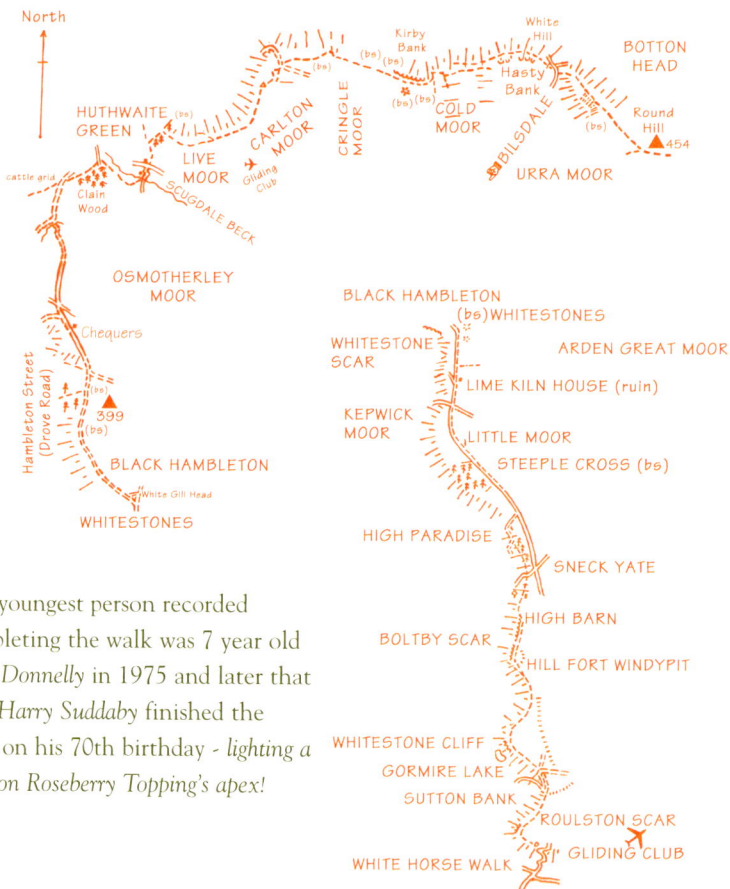

The youngest person recorded completing the walk was 7 year old *Sean Donnelly* in 1975 and later that year *Harry Suddaby* finished the walk on his 70th birthday - *lighting a cake on Roseberry Topping's apex!*

NEWTON UNDER ROSEBERRY

ROSEBERRY
TOPPING
320

GRIBDALE GATE
COATE MOOR

CAPT.
COOK'S
MONUMENT
324

KILDALE

WARREN
MOOR

BATTERSBY
MOOR

TIDY
BROWN
HILL

BURTON
HOWE

Incline
Top

BLOWITH
CROSSING

441   (bs)

Cockayne Head

North

Kirby
Bank
(bs)

(bs)

White
Hill

BOTTON
HEAD

Hasty
Bank

HUTHWAITE (bs)
GREEN

CARLTON MOOR

CRINGLE
MOOR

(bs)(bs) COLD
MOOR

BILSDALE

Round
Hill
(bs)

454

LIVE
MOOR

Gliding
Club

URRA MOOR

cattle grid

Clain
Wood

SCUGDALE BECK

OSMOTHERLEY
MOOR

BLACK HAMBLETON
(bs) WHITESTONES

Chequers

WHITESTONE
SCAR

ARDEN GREAT MOOR

LIME KILN HOUSE (ruin)

Hambleton Street
(Drove Road)

(bs)

399
(bs)

KEPWICK
MOOR

LITTLE MOOR

STEEPLE CROSS (bs)

BLACK HAMBLETON

White Gill Head

HIGH PARADISE

WHITESTONES

SNECK YATE

HIGH BARN

BOLTBY SCAR

HILL FORT WINDYPIT

WHITESTONE CLIFF

GORMIRE LAKE

SUTTON BANK

ROULSTON SCAR

GLIDING CLUB

WHITE HORSE WALK

PREFACE

In early August 1993 a team of us including the author attempted the crossing of the Lyke Wake Walk. On this our first occasion we were almost completely unprepared for the challenge which had to be completed within 24 hours. Over fifteen hours and many miles later we arrived at the finish line almost completely exhausted after a very memorable trip. *We promised ourselves that one day we would return and complete the walk in a more dignified fashion!*

On the 1st August *(Yorkshire Day & White Rose Day)* in 1999 we returned to the North Yorkshire Moors after several years of walking experience. This time, we decided to attempt the south to north route of the little known *White Rose Challenge Walk*. The distances between the Lyke Wake Walk and the White Rose Walk are very similar *(the latter is 40 miles)*. We were lucky to have the same team with us on this second challenge walk and also the benefit of a very warm weekend.

My memory of the White Rose Walk is one of stunning countryside, arduous hill climbs and a lot of laughs!

We were joined on this occasion by two ladies, Dawn Peters and my wife, Kim Jones who were training for the New York Marathon later that year. Their previous training had obviously paid off because they were the first two members of the party to reach the summit of Roseberry Topping on the second day.

The terrain of the White Rose Walk and the training for a challenge walk must be taken seriously but at the end of the day you are also meant to have fun! It is with this in mind that Crystal Peaks has actively supported the White Rose Walk as a means of raising funds for the very worthy White Rose Children's Charity and the Centre is very proud to be associated with both.

I wish you every success in your attempt to complete the White Rose Challenge Walk and I certainly hope that you enjoy it just as much as we did.

Kind regards,

Chris

CGD Jones
Centre Manager, Crystal Peaks Shopping Centre, Sheffield

FOREWORD

by Geoff Myers C.B.E., President
White Rose Children's Charity

John Buttery J.P. Chairman & Audrey Wright Administrator,
White Rose Children's Charity

The founding of White Rose Children's Charity was brought about on the early retirement of a group of executives, managers and staff of a national transportation company. Having enjoyed their respective careers it was considered that some time could be dedicated to assist children and young people who were less fortunate. The focus was to be on those with cancer, leukaemia and special needs. The main criteria in the organisation of the charity was to ensure there would be no person whatever involved with the running of the charity who would receive financial reward. It was to commence, and remain as, a true charity.

Our mission statement is: *"To promote any charitable purpose anywhere in the world for the benefit of children and young people and in particular, but without limitation, the relief of sickness and the relief of poverty"*

By following our beliefs many thousands of youngsters have been the beneficiaries of the fund raising activities of many groups of people who see children as their future.

The charity has provided thousands of pounds of practical aid to relieve hunger, distress and poverty in places such as Albania, the Balkans, Chernobyl, India, Eastern Europe, Mozambique, Ethiopia and nearer home, children with special needs have been the recipients of gifts and services to a better life style.

An aspiration to provide a permanent long term facility was realised on the purchase of a holiday bungalow at Filey on the East Yorkshire Coast where children undertaking treatment or recuperating from cancer and leukaemia can spend some pleasurable days. It is also a location where teachers and carers of children with special needs can explore their difficulties and life's traumas in a setting which they regard as a holiday; for many this is an opportunity not readily available in their own environment.

Our desire and objective is to continue our work on a strictly voluntary basis to provide as much help possible to those less fortunate than ourselves.

We would hope that the readers of the "White Rose Challenge Walk" will in some way assist us to continue this invaluable contribution to future generations of those in need.

Please give a thought, undertake a task to ensure "White Rose" can receive funding for the future.

Thank you for your help.

G. Myers

Geoff Myers C.B.E. President

White Rose Children's Aid (International) Charity
23 Teesdale Road, Ridgeway, Sheffield S12 3XH
Registered Charity No.1036377
Telephone: 0114 248 8799 Facsimile: 0114 248 8799

THE WHITE ROSE CHALLENGE WALK

Ordnance Survey   Outdoor Leisure 26
1:25 000 2 1/2 in to 1 mile - 4 cm to 1 km   North York Moors - Western Area

The walk starts at the Forestry Commission car park called 'White Horse Bank' managed by Forestry Enterprise with toilets and a Visitors Centre only 2 miles away at Sutton Bank (*but you'll get there soon enough anyway!*).

KILBURN

Comes from the medieval *'Kylebourne'*, meaning settlement by the *'cool stream'*. The beck at Kilburn soon becomes the River Kyle further along and the village has stood the test of time . . . still being 1 mile long and $1/2$ a mile wide - just as it was in the Doomsday Book. There's also a pretty Norman Church of the Blessed Virgin Mary which dates from 1120-30 A.D.

*In Loving Memory
John Hodgson
Blessed Virgin Mary
Churchyard, Kilburn.*

THE WHITE HORSE OF KILBURN

The famous White Horse of Kilburn is a equine gargantuan. It's a imprint that took 30 volunteers 2 months to complete. It was marked out in 1857 and completed on that year's Mischievous Night

4th November by local village school master for thirty years, John Hodgson and his pupils (*legend has it, he and his accomplices were paid in barrels of beer!*) 'on the initiative of a wealthy London grocer Thomas Taylor, a native of Kilburn' and was subsequently cut into the turf at Low Town Brow. On Hodgson's gravestone

it says '*The plan is now in the York Museum*'. It was commissioned by Taylor perhaps because of his love of the ancient chalk down figure at Uffington - another White Horse, in Berkshire, or simply because Yorkshire didn't have one of it's own or maybe perhaps because it's a 1 in 4 scarp and would be a shame to waste it (*ask any outdoor advertising person*) - nobody really knows and there's even rumours it could be associated with White Mare Crag - just to the north. Anyway, one thing's for certain, it can be seen for miles (*some say 70*) - even from the A1 (M) you'll catch a glimpse. The story goes, 20 people can picnic on its eye but, you're more than likely to get shoo'ed off by the management and members of the Kilburn White Horse Association for trespassing hence the notice... '*Do Not Walk On The White Horse*' itself sign.

They'll tell you it's also nay-easy to maintain, as the substrate is a limestone mud so you'd be forgiven for thinking its chalk, in reality, it's white paint with some chalk chippings on the surface - for added whiteness! It's the job of the K.W.H.A. to stabilise the surface and keep to the horse's original shape including colour, checking the drainage and limiting the erosion. Phew! Why? Because rumour has it in 1896 a rain and hail storm nearly erased it! In 1925 the readers of the Yorkshire Evening Post subscribed to a restoration fund and with the residue of £100 invested '*to provide for triennial grooming of the figure*'.

It was again restored for £6,000 in 1968. Statistically the 2 acre White Horse measures imperially 314 feet by 228 feet high or metrically 96 metres long and 70 metres high. *From huge horses to miniature mice . . .*

ROBERT THOMPSON

Kilburn is famous for something else man made too, apart from large limestone white equines, small wooden mice! It was here in his appropriate half timbered Elizabethan house that traditional carpenter Robert Thompson lived and worked.

He was born in 1876 and his timber career started as the village wheelwright then he plied his trade as a self taught wood carver of (latterly) some repute. Robert's now known the world over as the famous *'Mouseman of Kilburn'*. He worked here with his adze (not a plane, but originally a mediaeval tool for taking chunks out of ships timbers) in English Oak, carving classic English styles based on his own idea's and 17th century furniture, right up until his death in 1955.

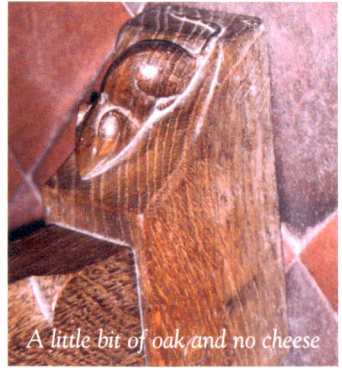

A little bit of oak and no cheese

From York Minster to Westminster Abbey, Helmsley to Kilburn, church carving was his speciality - and all locations contain evidence of his distinctive trade mark - a little mouse - hence *'we're all as poor as church mice'* a comment reputedly said by one of his craftsmen on the state of all their finances. There's even one on a gate in Robin Hood's Bay, so get the cheese and trap out, it'll probably be the most expensive mouse you'll ever buy!

Robert Thompson's Cottage & Old Workshop

Tourist trap & squeaky clean - The Mouseman Visitor's Centre

FORRESTERS ARMS HOTEL

The carver's showroom is near the Forresters Arms Hotel, in which is a seat commemorating George VI and Elizabeth and guess what - it has a mouse on it too. How's that for linking both together! Just look across the road for the naturally maturing stacked planks of oak being latted, stored and gently seasoned from movement over time.

A Forestry Commission 'White Horse Walk' plaque shows the location of place names and tells of Druid Priests holding sacrifices!

o.k. so watch out for . . . . aircraft !

THE WHITE ROSE CHALLENGE WALK

Enough local knowledge and history, on with the challenge . . climb the stairs and then snake the foot path on top of the White Horse. Once on the path you'll see the car park below on the left with the most stunning and dramatic views of the Plain of York and the Pennine Chain. Forestry Commission woodlands extend along and below the escarpment edge. The walk follows the Cleveland Way between the escarpment face and the private airfield used by the Yorkshire Gliding Club which was established in 1931.

The immediate area and surroundings has had a long and varied history giving rise to many strange place names such as Hood Hill - where Robin Hood is supposed to have fought his last battle, Happy Valley, Devils Parlour, Hell Hole, Fairies Parlour and the Thief's Highway.

A sign says "Beware Low Flying" - low flying what though? You can't miss the fluorescent wind sock and the array of gliders as you pass to the right hand side of the Yorkshire Gliding Club at Sutton Bank. It's an ideal location for gliding because the escarpment edge provides a band of rising air which the glider pilot uses to keep airborne. This 1 in 4 was used for motor trials in the 1920's - the judge and jury are still out on that one as to who reached the top - if anyone!

9

Keeping on the path you'll see firstly a public footpath sign 'Ceveland Way/Sutton Bank' then a commemorative plaque.

Keep left at the fork to see a little further along a telescope strategically placed to gain a closer look at these wonderful views across the plains.

Another plaque informs you of Sutton Bank's height above sea level - 981 feet - presented and erected by the A.A. (*the motoring association not Alcoholics Anonymous!*).

Gormire Lake

Viewing from left to right, York, The Hawk Hills, Knaresborough Castle, Harrogate, The Pennines, Great Whernside, Jervaux Abbey, Thirsk, Bedale, Richmond, North Allerton and Gormire Lake. The first 6 miles of the footpath runs along the rim of Roulston Scar and cliffs passing the mysterious Lake Gormire with no outlet or inlet feeder stream, one of only two naturally formed lakes in Yorkshire.

Proceed along the path and you'll see some motorist deviations signs (black and white chevron's) for a sharp bend in the A170 road, cross it and bear left for 20 yards to rejoin the limestone footpath sign posted with yellow arrows and an acorn - it skirts the edge of the hill to view the beautiful Lake Gormire. The lake is surrounded by myth and magic - *but being bottomless what do you expect!*

Follow the well defined path and yet another telescope following the *'Cleveland Way/Sneck Yate'* signs!

'Teach tha' sen tyke' - that means illucidate yourself in the ways of the Yorkshire Language. Lesson One: Sneck Yate is pronounced Sneck Yat - yat means gate!

Passing through Garbutt Wood you'll see another great view of Lake Gormire and the path passes Whitestone Cliff. Your path is onward to a marker for *'Bridleway / Dialstone Farm'* pointing right, don't follow it, it's just for reference - you should be sticking to the many *'Cleveland Way/Sneck Yate'* signs!

Later you'll pass through a gate to High Barn.

To the east is Hambleton Down or Hambleton Race Ground, here, in it's 'hay-day' (*which was the 18th century + note appropriate use of horsey wording!*), between 1602 and 1811, racing took place at one of the finest racecourses in England. Thorough-bred horses were trained and raced here, you can still see stables nearby and limestone turf gallops that cross the way. The location of the weighing machine is marked by a large stone opposite Dialstone Farmhouse - the name coming supposedly from the dial of the gauge for a jockey's weigh-in or perhaps part of the judges measuring equipment - it's inscribed 1705.

Two Inns, the Hambleton and Dialstone (*now the afore mentioned farm*) catered for the aristocracy of the day and also the less opulent cattle drovers who would have been imbibing the ale, wine and spirits. One can only giggle at both 'classes' being side by side!

Whitestone Cliff or White Mare Crag

High Barn

Proof, as if you needed it, of the prosperity that came in 1719 as 31 runners entered for *'His Majesty's Gold Cup'* and the winner *'Bonny Black'* owned by the Duke of Rutland was duly presented by non other than King George I. Queen Anne also presented gold cups and plates to winners here with annual races worth up to 100 guineas each. Even Daniel Defoe, writer of *'Robinson Crusoe'*, visited the races in 1742 and commented on their excellence.

It's demise was due to near-by York finally galloping off with *'The Hundred Guineas'* in 1755 but you may still spot the odd one or two four legged friends today having a work out - gee-up!

Over a stile to cross the Boltby road at Sneck Yate Bank and follow a gravel path sign posted *'Cleveland Way/Osmotherly 9 miles'*. The track leads through two gates to a tarmaced track, keep right and ignore the temptation to go into Boltby Forest at the fork (with a large green Forestry sign) onwards to High Paradise Farm a beautiful long building with a courtyard and two barns, keep on to the Cleveland Way sign, then turn left, taking you to Hambleton Drove Road.

It's a hard tractor track! Seeing a mixed woodland in front of you proceed though. Yes, now it <u>is</u> Boltby Forest *(don't follow the blue arrow forward - it'll take you on a footpath straight across Dale Town Common!)* Emerge and follow the Cleveland Way sign shortly, coming to a boundary stone with a level marker - Steeple Cross.

Further along a boundary marker C T 1770 appears and yet another boundary marker C T 1770 again claims you take notice of CT's land boundaries - or else!

THE HAMBLETON DROVE ROAD

It's an ancient way that splits at Steeple Cross to go southward onto York whilst the south easterly track goes down Stocking Lane then onto Malton and further afield like the Humber, Lincolnshire and Norfolk. Cattle droving is the early equivalent of our fridge freezer - only mobile. It's literally *'meat on the hoof'* without the fume's of your Uncle Jim's Ford Transit van. The cattle of entire families were entrusted to one man - he had to avoid the cattle getting lost, suffering disease, weight loss and still at the end of the day get a good price for his differing herds.

Trespassers take notice, this is one of C.T.'s boundary stones

'Moorland' road signs courtesy of the Highways Department **No.1** *Evel Knevel*

This route, an ancient highway, the Hambleton Drove Road, was used most notably in the 18th and 19th centuries by Northumbrian and Scottish 'businessmen' good at being trust worthy for their clients, walking, talking and of course, negotiating - whilst bringing their cattle south to fairs and markets in tact. They favoured this ridge way route as turnpikes had expensive tolls and some routes had costly toll bridges to boot, but they needed services like farriers and the odd ale house (*surprise, surprise!*) - enter the *'Chequers Inn'* and *'Lime Kiln Inn'* (*even Dialstone House /Farm/Inn*). Sadly Lime Kiln Inn is in ruins today but indeed thought to be more associated with drovers for their creature comforts than that of the nearby lime quarries, pack horses and lime burning.

Go past National Cycling Network Marker No. 65.

If you're interested in waymarkers and boundary stones, there are two just to the right - i) Osmotherley Road North ii) CT (again!) and finally one on our track - Grey Hall Stone.

And at a minor road, no not a football result: simply Swainby 5 Middlesbrough 22 on the blue markers.

Carry straight on to/in/or passed the old cattle drovers paradise 'Chequers Inn' at Slape Stones. It's situated on the Hawnby Road and it is said, for over two hundred years the Chequers had a turf fire glowing constantly day and night. Note the sign outside: *"Be not in haste: Step in and taste; Ale tomorrow for nothing"* - because tomorrow never comes - it's always yesterday's today! Sadly it's not an Inn anymore - it's now a farm and a very nice tea room and small shop to rest your feet.

Now a choice . . .

for speedsters *(see hares)* pass Chequers and Solomans Temple and head up the High Lane track to the Ford at Sheep Wash - crossing a footbridge *(to your left a moorland car park for motorists and perhaps your support party)* joining and advancing onwards via Quarry Lane appropriately passing the old workings to finally reach Scarth Nick cattle grid - this route completely by-passes Osmotherly.

for pleasure crusiers *(see tortoise)* grub and pub seekers and 'the over two day types', from 'Chequers' follow the tarmaced road round and over the cattle grid then turn right at the foot path sign into a field keeping the hedge on your right, through the squeeze stile down to White House Farm

This sign hung outside Chequers when it was a cattle drovers inn. Restored by Osmotherly Society 1984.

following the Cleveland Way signs. Over a stile descend the valley to Cod Beck, over a gated wooden footbridge over Cod Beck - ford the stream (*climb every mountain*) and up the steeped or is that stepped paths (*both!*) through Middlestye Bank to open pasture via a kissing gate. Cheat and use Osmotherly's Parish Church Tower as a direction finder for Back Lane. Enter it via another kissing gate and 4 squeeze stiles or sheep snecks (*I think*) taking you through a hedged lane leading to St. Anne's Cottage (No.16), the Methodist Chapel and a passage-way that leads into the village square and beyond.

this sign was in the field at the side of White House Farm!

OSMOTHERLY

Welcome to Asmundrelac

Da daaa! You've reached Osmotherly or the more romantic Asmundrelac in the Doomsday Book of 1086 - that's like the *"Norman Times"*, a broadsheet of the day.

Asmund is Norse and this was Asmund's Clearing. 'As' changed to 'Os' and suitably linked with the local legend of Prince Oswy. The story goes, the Prince of Northumberland was taken to Roseberry Topping by his Mum to avoid drowning on a certain cursed day - only for her to find him face down dead in a hill side spring, Roseberry Well.
So watch your step later at ye olde Toppyne!

Osmotherly, a small market village, once used the power of Cod Beck you've just crossed for weaving and bleaching. With jet mines and alum quarries all around, Osmotherly helped to provide accommodation for these transient workers, so agriculture and industry lived side by side making it a popular place to live and work during the 18th and 19th centuries. With it's market cross and '*five stone pillars*' supporting the barter slab - it's been used as a market stall, a coffin resting place and has even had John Wesley putting it to good use many times as an open air stone pulpit for his Methodist preaching, *but then again, there's not many places he hasn't been!*

Our route continues northward ascending up 'North End' (*towards Scarth Nick - sign posted 2 1/2 miles and Swainby*) and turning left into the marked Ruebury Lane.

We follow this track around Ruebury Hill passing Chapel Wood Farm through a kissing gate. Sadly, we miss viewing the only Carthusian house in Yorkshire (*one of only nine*) and the best preserved - Mount Grace Priory (on the left) and the annual pilgrimage site of the early 16th century Shrine of Our Lady of Mount Grace - Lady's Chapel (on the right). We proceed through three fields to enter Arncliffe Wood/South Wood and take the right fork following a Cleveland Way marker.

After a short forest section you 'aim' for the television, radio and communications transmitter mast of British Telecom on Beacon Hill by going through South Wood. You'll see a Ordnance Survey trig point (S. 4413) marking the 982 feet (299 metres) summit of the Hill and it's also famous for the 'would be' '*dirgers*' of the Lyke Wake Walk. They get *'under starters orders'* here for the famous Potto farmer's walk - the Bill Cowley classic 40+ miler to complete the Osmotherly to Ravenscar challenge. The crossing needs to be completed within 24 hours or under to become part of the elite Lyke Wake Club - Lyke for the corpse, Wake for the celebration of the dead and Club - a weapon to beat yourself up with for doing it in the first place - *I'm speaking from personal experience here!* We'll follow and share this route for about the next 10 miles.

Coffin badge of honour

Emerge onto the National Trust's Scarth Wood Moor along the well trodden path over a track with a L.L.W. (Lyke Wake Walk) stone marker leading to Coalmire Lane and the famous Scarth Nick cattle grid (*note the 39 mls sign for the L.L.W.*) - both *hare* and *tortoise* unite at this point.

You proceed into the plantation called Clain Wood - by skirting it's edge around Round Hill. You'll hopefully have a fine view of the Vale of Cleveland maybe seeing the Pennines, Nidderdale, Wensleydale and Swaledale.

Follow the path inside Clain Wood but at the first fork take a left (*acorn marked*) descending down the forest section contouring the side of Scugdale Beck. There's two Cleveland Way signs and a gate to go through before going over the Beck's footbridge spanning the stream - and

1 down 39 miles to go for the LLW

WHITE ROSE CHALLENGE WALK

Mini Pull-Out

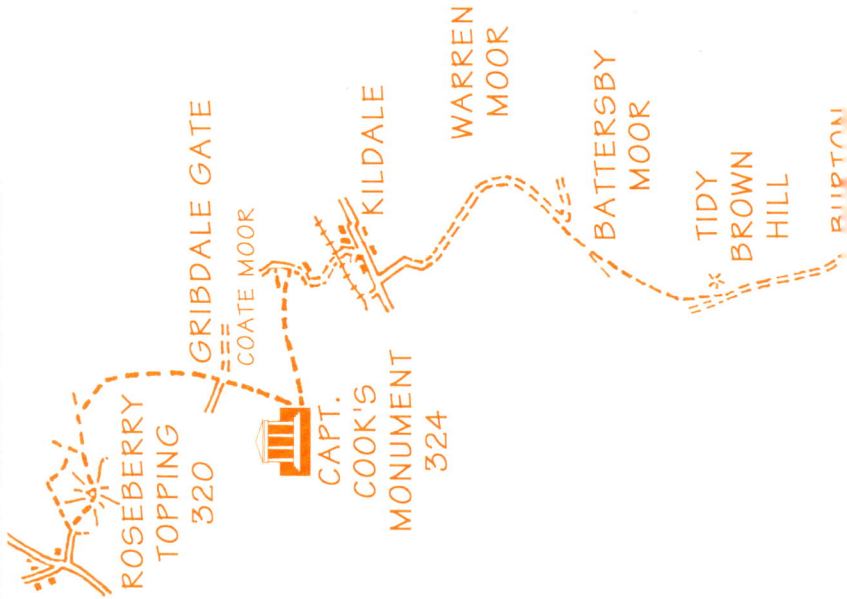

NEWTON UNDER ROSEBERRY

ROSEBERRY TOPPING 320

GRIBDALE GATE

COATE MOOR

CAPT. COOK'S MONUMENT 324

KILDALE

WARREN MOOR

BATTERSBY MOOR

TIDY BROWN HILL

BURTON

O.S. GRID REFERENCES S-N

Location	Grid Ref.	Miles	Time
White Horse	514812	00	06.15
Sutton Bank Top	514829	01	06.30
Sneck Yate	507875	05	07.30
Whitestones	491932	09	08.30
Thimbley Moor Viewpoint	479958	10	08.45
Soloman's Temple	474973	11	09.00
Sheep Wash	471994	13	09.30
Swainby Bank-Cattle Grid	473004	14	10.00
Scugdale Beck	493005	16	10.45
Carlton Moor Trig	519026	20	12.00
Hasty Bank	573033	25	14.00
Bloworth Crossing	616015		
Battersby Crag & Moor	605062	30	15.45
Baysdale Gate	611070	32	7.00
Quarry at Baysdale Road	609084	34	17.30
Kildale	608094	35	18.00
Bankside Farm	605101	36	18.45
Gribdale Gate	592101	38	19.30
Newton Under Roseberry	571126	40	20.30

yet another footbridge - if the water level is high! Take a left up the track to Hollin Hill Farm and cottages at Huthwaite Green where you should find a telephone and post box - *civilisation at last!* Across through the gate going north east with the fence on your right eventually the path forks but keep left on the edge of Live Moor Plantation and head for Live Moor by climbing the steep stone cobbled steps. *Phew!*

Follow the well defined path passing waymarker "A" to the Ordnance Survey trig point (S. 4421) at the highest point on Carlton Moor, Carlton Bank, 1338 feet (408 metres). If you look closely in the middle of the photograph below, in the distance, you'll see Roseberry Topping our destination. You'll have just passed the grass runway of the Teeside & Newcastle Gliding Club.

A up!

After crossing the Raisdale Road, if you've time for a little exploration, very doubtful, unless you're doing the Challenge over two days, slightly to the east of the road is the *'Three Lords Stone'* where three local landlord's boundaries met: i) the *Duncombe* family of Helmsley ii) *Marwood* of Busby Hall, and iii) *Ailesbury* of Snilesworth. There's also a unique *'underground'* café called the *'Lord Stones Cafe'*

Ye Olde Toppyne!

built into the hillside early in the 20th century. It's a good place for any White Rose Challenge Walker(s) to stop and get an alcoholic drink - if you buy some food, thanks to the proprietor's license! *It also has toilets too.*

You'll be following in the footsteps of many a Lyke Wake Walk'er, Cleveland Way'er & Coast to Coast'er.

If you didn't divert - the well trodden path crosses the Raisdale Road and up onto Cringle *(Circle)* Moor. At the edge of Kirkby Bank you'll pass a seat, standing stone and plate as a tribute to office worker Alec

Lord Stones Cafe

Falconer *'Rambler'* 1884 - 1968 a highly respected member of the Middlesbrough Rambling Club and founder of the Cleveland Way - in those days, it was called the Moors and Coast Path.

The Wainstones

Over the summit of Cold Moor follow the Cleveland Way marker over a stile and on to the Wainstones which are a rock climbers paradise - *crampons and guide ropes at the ready!* A huge outcrop of bare stones - their name could be a derivation of the Saxon word 'wan ion' meaning to wail or to weep, this mournful cry or lament *(appropriate for the Lyke Wake Walk route)* could be caused by wind blowing through them, building up the folklore legend of wailing stones. The route continues down to Hasty Bank *(Norse for horse)* descending right down the edge of Spring House Wood to reach the B1257. This 'B' road links Helmsley with Stokesley.

Cross over and through a gate called *"Haggs Gate"*, up on to Carr Ridge over Urra Moor - you're on your way up to Round Hill at Botton Head *(Norse for steep)* which stands at 1489 feet (454 metres) - it's the highest point on the North York Moors *and the Cleveland Hills for that matter!* You'll see trig point No. 2988 with nearby standing stone, the Hand Stone - it says "THIS IS THE WAY TO KIRBY" with the hand pointing eastward whilst northward "THIS IS THE WAY TO STOXLA".

This plate & seat in memory of Alec Falconer "Rambler"

Reach the summit and then it's all down hill into Kildale - *that's a promise*.

Passed the summit is another unique boundary stone to watch out for - *'The Face Stone'* or *Face Stone Cross* which was mentioned in the 1642 book *'Perambulations on the Streete Way'* which is about the east-west paved trod featuring *'the bounder called Faceston'*. It's believed to be of Celtic origin.

Through Cockayne Head on to Bloworth Crossing - locals call it Blowith or Blowath. For 68 years 1861-1929 the crossing had manned gates for safety. Ahead of you is the eastern section of the dismantled track of Rosedale Ironstone Railway first opened in 1861 by the North Eastern Railway Company for iron ore mineral transportation from the Rosedale mines to be taken for smelting to Teeside and Durham. It finally closed on 8th June 1929 - when the mining boom was over.

This is where we bid a fond adios to the classic Lyke Wake Walk route which we have been following since Osmotherly. Both the Cleveland Way and Lyke Wake Walk routes next join up at Hawsker Bottom.

We turn left (*northerly*) taking the Cleveland Way signs toward Incline Top seeing green metal gates and a stone marker heading for two standing stones. The smaller standing stone or ancient waymarker has a personal name, simply called *"Jenny Bradley"* marked on O.S. maps as Cross near the 421 metre mark.

The 'Face Stone'

The second, taller stone has carvings on three sides: 1) SIR W FOWELS, 2) T.A. 1768 3) F1838 indicating landowner agreements and owners initials for boundaries - here it's the afore mentioned Sir W. Fowels the 8th Baronet of the Ingleby Estate who died in 1845.

On route you'll pass nine grouse butts starting with - guess what - No. 9 !

On to the Bronze Age burial site of Burton Howe passing four burial mounds.

Much further on still is another *"hand stone"* a signpost relic from the 18th century. It has

Hand Stone' - Dated 1757

carved stone pointing palms, *(have some small change ready to place in the rim under the capping stone to maintain an old custom of gaining good luck for you and purchasing food and drink for the less fortunate and weary traveller that comes along the way later)* and shows the way to *"Stoxla"* (Stokesley) *"Kirby"* and *"Hemsley"* (Helmsley).

Kildale Post Office making Harry a man of letters

Ahead of you is Ingleby Greenhowe and Tidy Brown Hill with it's tumulus and finally Battersby Moor. Go through the metal gate and over Battersby Moor crossing Cross Dyke to reach the road at Bayside Farm. Park Dyke to your right is believed to be a medieval deer park complete with earthen mound, walled enclosure and dyke.

Follow the road down into Kildale village turning right at the T junction. You'll see a phone box on your right *'to phone home'* and the Post Office belonging to Harry & Glen Mucklow's *'Kildale Village Store'* - I've begged them for sandwiches, tea, coffee and a lift many a time and they've never said 'no' - *yet!*

KILDALE

Originally an ancient settlement the moorland sandstone-block village of Kildale is better known as an 'estate', set in the valley of the River Leven and has, over the last 900 years been in the hands of three families - it only has three rights of way on old O.S. maps to prove it - so boundaries have never ever changed! Almost all the houses and farms are still owned and maintained by the estate - keeping a real sense of tradition and community spirit.

The village was originally situated on a ex-moated manor house of 12th Century origin - (*some books refer to it being a motte and bailey castle*) belonging to the Percy family (*Percy Rigg and Percy Cross on the North York Moors*) later to be replaced by a mediaeval manor house of which a few stones remain. It's prosperity was again due to the mining of iron ore, jet, whinstone and of weaving mills. One of which, Bleach Mill was washed away over 160 years ago by a dam collapse. Bleach Mill Farm now stands on that westerly site today. In the swinging '60's *'Beeching's Axe'* a British Railways henchman - missed chopping the Esk Valley railway line between Middlesbrough and Whitby and therefore Kildale still retains it's station. The church, St. Cuthbert's is reached by crossing the footbridge. Renovation of it in 1867 saw Viking relics dug up from beneath the floor, like swords and battleaxes - *not surprising as it's stood on sites of various building successions since Saxon times!*

Cook's Monument

Follow the Cleveland Way marker past Glebe Cottage which is a Café and Tea Room with a sign saying *'Muddy Boot's Welcome'* & *'Thirsty Doggy Stop'*.

Leaving Kildale the path descends along the road to the right marked with national speed limit signs. After passing under the railway bridge and crossing the River Leven, follow the road over the cattle grid ascending up through Bankside Cottage (*Bed & Breakfast*) and then Bankside Farm - at the top of the steep bank, turn left signposted *'Gribdale 2 miles'* on the forestry track of Coate Moor Woods.

At the intersection of track follow the *'Cleveland Way'* signpost through the forest to the clearing of Easby Moor to Captain Cook's Monument by way of a flagstone pavement.

Captain James Cook RN., F.R.S. (1728-1779) Mariner, Navigator and Explorer.

This is your life . . .

He was born in Marton-in-Cleveland in the North Riding of Yorkshire, 3 miles south of Middlesbrough on 27th October 1728. Middlesborough's Stewart Park is now on the site of the young James Cook's two roomed thatched cottage. There's another voyage of discovery there too - The Captain Cook Birthplace Museum 1º/12' which features interactive displays and original artifacts. Also, in 1858 an iron master called H.W.F. Bolckow erected a granite vase to mark the exact spot. Finally, Marton gained another momento in the shape of an obelisk *(a stone memorial)* to be placed on the village green with thanks from Point Hicks Hill,

Victoria, *(a replica to the one placed there already)* to mark the First Great Voyage of Exploration, as Point Hicks was the first land mark Cook's crew sighted in Australia from the Endeavour on 19th April 1770. His childhood home from 1736, at age 8, was at Airyholme Farm, Great Ayton, a village with the River Leven linking High and Low Green flowing beside the long street. The Lord of the Manor was Mr. Thomas Skottowe of Ayton Hall and James's father was bailiff to him. Mr. Skottowe paid for Jame's schooling. The school in which he was educated *(and excelled at mathematics)* is the Michael Postgate School, in High Street, founded in 1704, he was taught there from 1736-1741. It's now the Captain Cook Schoolroom Museum.

The James Cook Sculpture by Nicholas Dimbleby on High Green shows Cook at 16 years old. If you want to see the bricks and mortar 1755 version of his father's stone built house in Great Ayton you'll need wings! It was bought in 1933 by W. Russell Grimwade when it came up for sale and it's now emigrated to Fitzroy Gardens, Melbourne, shipped out in 1934 stone by stone and reassembled. Cook left school at about 12/13 to work with his father and brother on the farm which he waves goodbye to at 16 to start his career as an apprentice grocer / draper / haberdasher to a Mr William Sanderson, just up the coast in the picturesque village of Staithes, he was a local merchant - it lasted eighteen months. Because he was working close by the 'Cod & Lobster Inn' - I'm sure he'd see net mending, fish salting and gutting or be listening to sea shantys, sea faring and smugglers tales, no doubt! He was also reputed to be living near the pub in what's now known as "Cooks Cottage". The young Cook was reputably idle and did indeed get flogged by his master Sanderson, once for 'mislaying a shilling' (12 old pennies), anyway a taste for the sea beckoned and the rest, as they say, is history. Sanderson recommends Cook to a friend he knows in Whitby, and in 1746 he went there, where he was taught maritime lore

under a ship owner of colliers and Quaker named John Walker - his red bricked, elegant 17th century Georgian house, and Cook's attic lodgings are situated in Whitby's Grape Lane - it's now the basis of the Captain Cook Memorial Museum (founded in 1987 - their web site is www.cookmuseumwhitby.co.uk). This is where Cook slept and studied as a young sailor with the sloping backyard appropriately leading down to the River Esk. It's called 'the house on the harbour, with windows on the world'. 'Cats' or flat bottomed wooden ships (built at nearby Fishburn & Langborne Shipyard) carried coal from the Tyne to the Thames and this was Cook's first experience of sea faring as an 'indentured apprentice' to Captain Walker for three years. His first sailing was on Walker's 450 ton sturdy Whitby collier, the "Freelove".

In 1755 Walker wanted to commission Cook to command his own collier the 'Friendship' - Cook declined, instead choosing the Royal Navy as an ordinary seaman. Cook was on the Pembroke, a sixty four gunner, in charge of navigation, helping to convoy General Wolfe's troops to Canada when he charted the St. Lawrence River to Quebec. With his help the city was captured in 1759.

The Newfoundland coast-line was next to be surveyed by Cook with his skill seeing him join numerous survey expeditions in the Atlantic until finally in command of his own famously named ships, the HMS Discovery, HMS Resolution and HM Bark Endeavour, all Whitby built "Cats" (today they might be named Felix, Tom and Sylvester). The Endeavour was originally called the Earl of Pembroke but was renamed when purchased by the Admiralty for our hero's first voyage. She was built in 1764, weighed 368 tons and was 106 feet long.

"To Strive To Seek, To Find and not to Yield"

1st August 1768 - 12th June 1771	First Voyage	- HM Bark Endeavour
13th July 1772 - 30th July 1775	Second Voyage	- HMS Resolution
12th July 1776 - 4th October 1780	Third Voyage	- HMS Resolution*

* with Captain Clerke in command of Discovery

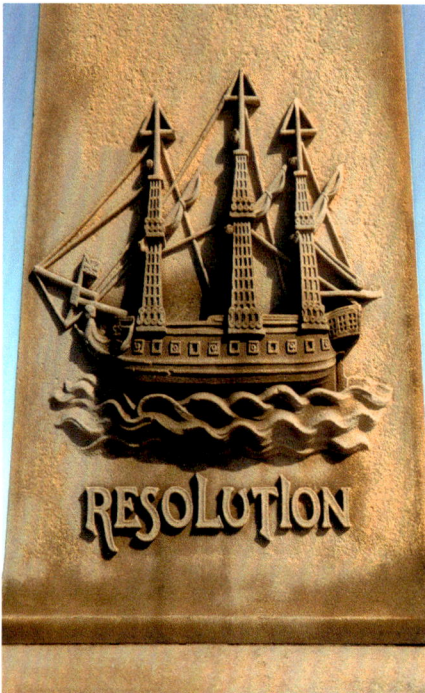

During these voyages of discovery Cook charted the coastlines of Australia and New Zealand, mapped unknown areas of the Pacific and even found time to develop a cure for scurvy! On 14th February, 1779, now Hawaii, then the Sandwich Islands (after Cook's patron John Montague, Earl of Sandwich), a shore party were attacked by angry natives after trying to demand the safe return of their 'ship's cutter' which had been stolen. Cook and a party of his men went ashore to unsuccessfully recover the boat. Cook was sadly clubbed and repeatedly stabbed to death along with two other Royal Marines. The remains of his body were ceremoniously buried

IN MEMORY OF
THE CELEBRATED CIRCUMNAVIGATOR
CAP.T JAMES COOK F.R.S.
A MAN IN NAUTICAL KNOWLEDGE INFERIOR TO NONE;
IN ZEAL PRUDENCE AND ENERGY SUPERIOR TO MOST.
REGARDLESS OF DANGER HE OPENED AN INTERCOURSE
WITH THE FRIENDLY ISLES AND OTHER PARTS
OF THE SOUTHERN HEMISPHERE.
HE WAS BORN AT MARTON OCT; 27.TH 1728
AND MASSACRED AT OWYHEE FEB; 14.TH 1779
TO THE INEXPRESSIBLE GRIEF OF HIS COUNTRYMEN.
WHILE THE ART OF NAVIGATION SHALL BE CULTIVATED
AMONG MEN, WHILE THE SPIRIT OF ENTERPRISE,
COMMERCE, AND PHILANTHROPY, SHALL ANIMATE
THE SONS OF BRITAIN, WHILE IT SHALL BE DEEMED
THE HONOUR OF A CHRISTIAN NATION TO SPREAD
CIVILIZATION AND THE BLESSINGS OF THE
CHRISTIAN FAITH AMONG PAGAN AND SAVAGE TRIBES.
SO LONG WILL THE NAME OF CAP.T COOK
STAND OUT AMONG THE MOST CELEBRATED AND
MOST ADMIRED BENEFACTORS OF THE HUMAN RACE.

AS A TOKEN OF RESPECT FOR;
AND ADMIRATION OF THAT GREAT MAN
THIS MONUMENT WAS ERECTED BY
ROBERT CAMPION ESQ.R OF WHITBY. A.D.1827

BY THE PERMISSION OF THE OWNER OF THE EASBY ESTATE
J. J. EMERSON ESQ.R IT WAS RESTORED IN 1895
BY THE READERS OF THE NORTH EASTERN DAILY GAZETTE.

at sea in Kealakekua Bay on the Kona Coast of Hawaii on 21st February, 1779. As a tribute to this great pioneer, standing 1000 feet above sea level is Captain Cook's Monument. Erected in 1827 on Easby Moor it stands 50 feet high or today's metric equivalent, 15.25 metres. The topping out ceremony was done on 27th October 1827 - the centenary of Captain James Cook's birth.

The foundation stone was laid on 12th July 1827 - the same day Cook set sail from Plymouth on his 'Third Voyage of Exploration', in 1776. From the Monument a broad flagged track heads north descending through Little Ayton Moor to the road at Gribdale Gate.

Crossing over just to the right you'll see the stepped footpath going directly up the ridge opposite at the side of a stone wall and forest toward the Great Ayton Moor.

You'll notice another boundary stone - T HR GA . Follow the path and signpost through a gate down to Roseberry Common ascending to the peak of Roseberry Topping - all 320 metres, 1056 feet.

Classed as Cleveland's *"Little Matterhorn"* Roseberry Topping is owned by the National Trust *(purchased in 1985)* and named after the sacred Danish God of Creation - 'Odin.' *'Odin's Hill'* or *Odin's Berg*, altered in the 12th Century to Othensberg, hence the village becoming *Newton under Ouesbergh* and eventually *Newton under Roseberry* a derivation. In the 17th century references were made to the peak as *"Osbury Toppyne"*. It has seen a varied and chequered history . . . as a 'unlit' warning beacon for any invasion by the Spanish Armada to having a bonfire lit on the summit in celebration of the coronation of Edward VII. In the late 1800's quarry men realised that beneath the sandstone cap was solid ironstone, not to miss an opportunity they gnawed away underneath it extracting the iron ore via an aerial ropeway. Alum, jet and road stone all followed but in either in 1912 or 1914 things got a little serious when the top collapsed into the mine workings. Unperturbed labour and toil continued until 1929 but eventually closed on uneconomic grounds. The views from the top are stunning - the North Sea, Durham, the Cleveland Plains and the Pennines all stretch out in front of you.

Literally a little worst for wear and battle scarred, Roseberry Topping is still standing - with you on it!

Touch the triangulation pillar and you've made it!

Roseberry Toppings revealed rear!

O.S. GRID REFERENCES S-N

Location	Grid Ref.	Miles	Time
White Horse	514812	00	06.15
Sutton Bank Top	514829	01	06.30
Sneck Yate	507875	05	07.30
Whitestones	491932	09	08.30
Thimbley Moor Viewpoint	479958	10	08.45
Soloman's Temple	474973	11	09.00
Sheep Wash	471994	13	09.30
Swainby Bank-Cattle Grid	473004	14	10.00
Scugdale Beck	493005	16	10.45
Carlton Moor Trig	519026	20	12.00
Hasty Bank	573033	25	14.00
Bloworth Crossing	616015		
Battersby Crag & Moor	605062	30	15.45
Baysdale Gate	611070	32	7.00
Quarry at Baysdale Road	609084	34	17.30
Kildale	608094	35	18.00
Bankside Farm	605101	36	18.45
Gribdale Gate	592101	38	19.30
Newton Under Roseberry	571126	40	20.30

Free Sponsorship Information Packs & Merchandise

Prior to setting off, a complete fund raising pack is freely available to gain much needed support and sponsorship for White Rose Children's Charity, or, on successful completion of 40 mile White Rose Challenge Walk an exciting range of merchandise is available; including sew on badges and official completion certificates. The range is ever increasing so, for an up to date list, please contact either:

Audrey Wright
White Rose Children's Charity
23 Teesdale Road, Ridgeway
Sheffield, South Yorkshire S12 3XH
t: 0114 248 8799
f: 0114 248 8799

Darryl Dawson
Connexions PR & Marketing
Willoughby House, St. Marys Road
Tickhill, South Yorkshire DN11 9JQ
t: 01302 759696
e: darryl@connexions.uk.net
w: www.connexions.uk.net

A brief report on any footpath changes, route modifications, start and finishing times and numbers crossing will help to compliment any revisions or amendments to further updated publications. Thanking you in advance!

Safety Notes

The White Rose Challenge Walk is full of surprises, around every corner there's something of interest for all ages - from giant horses to tiny mice, huge monuments to red grouse, mining to lost railways. The walk can be a real day's challenge - one of the best ever - but I'm biased. For the less strenuous trek, divide it into a two day excursion, perhaps with an overnight stay in Stokesley, both days will be distinctive and contrasting. It's steeped in history and you'll gain fleeting glimpses into the past - I've given you a snap shot into the terrain and life blood of the area, one you may come to love and research further. Although very gentle in some areas the White Rose Challenge Walk is demanding - particularly crossing the North Yorkshire Moors - there's a number of undulating steep slopes waiting for you, also prepare to encounter mud - 'bog trotting' as it's better known! Please ensure you have adequate clothing to keep you comfortable, warm and waterproofed - at rest you may need more layers than when you're on the move - so layer up. Have strong 'bedded-in' walking boots! Carry hats, gloves and spare warm clothing, a whistle and torch (as signals if help is needed), a survival bag and first aid kit. Take along extra energy giving food like dried fruit or chocolate and some spare emergency rations plus a a warm drink 'just in case' or simply to enjoy 'on the tops'. Route plan and be prepared to modify it as conditions along the way change and should never be taken for granted - mists descend very quickly, maps and compass are essential - as is the knowledge on how to use them both! Finally, plan for the number of daylight hours available.

If Things Go Wrong . . .

In an emergency, if you are delayed, inform your base or the Police as quickly as possible so that the Scarborough & District Search & Rescue Team is not called out unnecessarily.

If you have a casualty, give first aid and make sure breathing is unobstructed, dress wounds to prevent bleeding and keep the casualty warm, sheltered and safe from further injury - remember to protect yourself too.

Send for help. Dial 999 for the North Yorkshire Police and then request Mountain Rescue, giving full details including an accurate location (give a grid reference if possible).

The Moors Message

TREAD GENTLY Despite surviving all sorts of weather, the moors, their plants and animals are fragile and sensitive.

FENCES AND WALLS Keep some animals in and some out, use stiles or gates (and shut them).

FIRE Uncontrolled fires can devastate miles of moorland which may never fully recover. Don't start fires or drop cigarettes or matches.

LITTER Is dangerous as well as unsightly - please take it home.

DOGS Keep dogs on leads at all times. A loose dog running over the moors can be catastrophic for ground nesting birds, sheep and sometimes the dog itself.

NOISE Moorlands should be quiet places, try to keep it that way.

SAFETY Weather conditions can change quickly, are you fully equipped?

FOOTPATHS Are for feet. Bicycles may be ridden on bridleways. Motorcycles and other vehicles should stick to roads.

COURTESY The North York Moors is a home and place for work for many people. Please respect their privacy.

NOTES

NOTES

The White Rose Challenge Walk - First Edition Published in June 2004
© Text and Photographs, Darryl Dawson 2004
British Library cataloguing in publication data:
a catalogue record for this book is available from the British Library.
ISBN 0-9544937-0-2

COUNTRYSIDE COMMISSION

THE COUNTRY CODE

Enjoy the countryside and respect it's life and work
Guard against all risk of fire
Fasten all gates
Keep your dogs under close control
Keep to public paths across farmland
Use gates and stiles to cross fences, hedges and walls
Leave livestock, crops and machinery alone
Take your litter home
Help to keep all water clean
Protect wildlife, plants and trees
Take special care on country roads
Make no unnecessary noise.

USEFUL INFORMATION

Tourist Information Centres
Whitby 01947 602674
Pickering 01751 473791
Helmsley 01439 770173
Ravenscar 01723 870138
Great Ayton 01642 722835
Sutton Bank 01845 597426
The Moors Centre 01287 660654

Heritage Coast Ranger
The Moors Centre, Danby, Whitby, North Yorkshire
Tel: 01287 660654
www.northyorkmoors-npa.gov.uk

National Park Office 01439 770657

Youth Hostels Association
PO Box 11, Matlock, Derbyshire DE4 2ZXA
Tel: 01629 825850